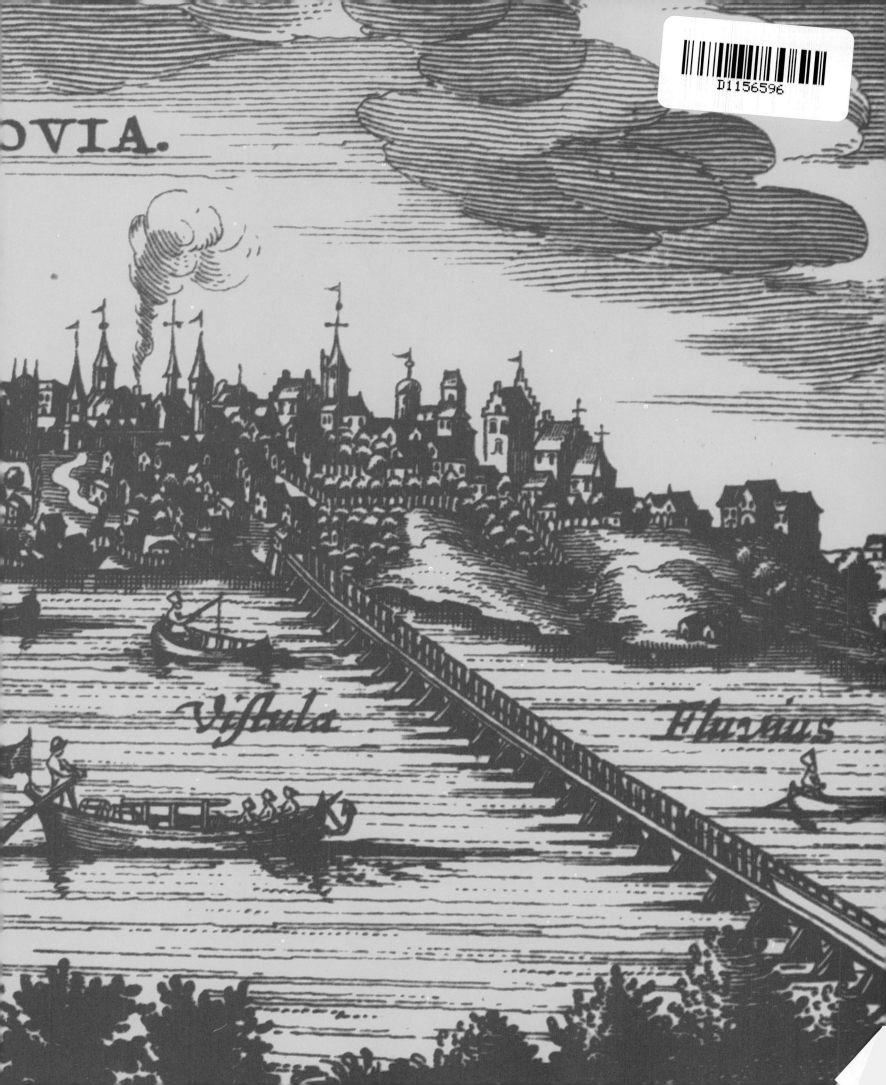

JAN MOREK

WARSAW
King's Road

Story by
Olgierd Budrewicz

**WYDAWNICTWA
ARTYSTYCZNE I FILMOWE**

TRANSLATED BY
ANDRE YAFFIE

GRAPHIC DESIGN
HUBERT HILSCHER

TECHNICAL EDITOR
HALINA SIWECKA

Text set by Wojtasiak–WOMIK, Warsaw
Printed in Austria by Milošević & Zanoff

ISBN 83-221-0625-4

Warsaw would not be there if it were not for King's Road. Some town of moderate interest would most probably develop in its place, one devoid of any firm historical roots or charm — a mere dot on the map.

The street known as King's Road is, strictly speaking, the road leading from the Royal Castle to the Łazienki Park. However, King's Road is usually made to include the Old Town (and therefore also the New Town), to the north, and the Belvedere, or even distant Wilanów, to the south.

Either way, the sequence of squares and streets running down New Town Market Square — the Barbican — Old Town Market Square — Świętojańska Street (St. John Str.) — Castle Square — Krakowskie Przedmieście (Kraków Suburb) — Nowy Świat (New World) — Trzech Krzyży (Three Crosses) Square — Ujazdowskie Avenue — has for years been considered the backbone of Warsaw's grandeur, historical evidence to successive turns of fate of Poland's capital and to the high rank of the metropolis. And it is around this area that the memories and emotions of the vast majority of Warsaw residents revolve. Poems are written about this several kilometre-long urban thoroughfare, songs are composed about it, and people yearn for it from all four corners of the world.

The overwhelming majority of other places of interest in Warsaw are located near Warsaw's equivalent of the Champs-Elysées, both gravitating towards it and complementing it at the same time.

King's Road is clearly associated with the last king of Poland, Stanisław August Poniatowski. Nevertheless, it became a "historic trail" centuries before. It is along here, and as early as the days of the Duchy of Mazovia, that the trade route from Czersk to Zakroczym ran. It gained importance well before the throne was moved to Warsaw, and kept its significance well after this historical event, and particularly under the Vasa Dynasty.

Crucial as King's Road has been to the layout of historical events on the Vistula, it has also imprinted itself on individual lives and minds of the Capital's residents.

Indeed, Warsaw would not be itself without King's Road.

☆

Warsaw's origins are difficult to pin down, and no decision about the time and place of its beginnings seems unquestionable.

It has been established that Warsaw's history goes back over seven centuries, and to the Old Town Market Square. In any case, it is known that, by the beginning of the 14th century, the market square and its immediate environs were fortified, i.e. they defended something that was, at the time, of some value.

We instinctively tend to shift the city's historical point of origin in time as well as in space. Indeed, one would like to push it back a hundred years or so, and move it several hundred metres to the north. Perhaps somewhere near what is now Traugutt Park, or perhaps even the Citadel. And while, walking southwards, one first enters the New Town and only then the Old Town, our imagination still conjures up images of Mazovian forests, that, in actual fact, vanished from this area long ago. Is this just fantasy? Very old structures that have been preserved and are doubtlessly authentic, still stand in the New Town. Prime evidence is found in the Church of the Visitation of Our Lady, erected one year after the Battle of Grunwald, i.e. in 1411. It has a belfry in local Gothic style.

The speculations of contemporary historians over the New Town, find a distant echo in the 19th-century chronicle by Franciszek Maksymilian Sobieszczański who maintained:

"Its location beyond the walls of Warsaw (...) and not within them can only be interpreted by the fact that the town was originally located elsewhere (...). It is hard to comprehend why the oldest Christian shrine and the first parish should have arisen off the centre of the main settlement, without having been included within the periphery of its walls".

This is like asking what came first – the hen or the egg. The place draws people's attention with its unique kind of magic. According to some reports, a small 12th-century church once stood here, allegedly dedicated to Saint George. The church no longer exists, but it has left traces in the name of the ancient Świętojerska (St. George's) Street. Quite plausible explanations have been forwarded that the same Saint George who killed the dragon provided inspiration for Warsaw's first coat of arms, before the Siren – the seductive but belligerent mermaid – arrived on the scene.

New Town Market Square with its side streets is one of the quietest areas in Warsaw. Cars had been banned from here, but a noisy cinema operated here for a while. The atmosphere of the place is reminiscent of small provincial towns in Italy.

A centuries-old legend says that the Church of Our Lady was put up where an old pagan shrine had once stood and that, nearby, Saint John's wreaths were thrown down the embankment at night to the Vistula down below, while Midsummer's Day bonfires were lit in the surrounding woods.

New Town Market Square used to look quite different, as a large town hall built of brick once stood here. It was praised by Adam Jarzębski, the author of the first (rhyming) guide to Warsaw: "Yonder a market splendid and proud, people so many, great is the crowd".

The façade of the Church of the Visitation of Our Lady

Later on, after the devastation of Swedish wars in the 17th century, when half the houses, including the town hall, fell prey to the roaring flames, the New Town was rebuilt and brought back to life. Shortly afterwards, King Zygmunt August built his first bridge over the river, right at the top of Mostowa (Bridge) Street. The street still exists today, charming and outdated with its uneven cobblestone pavings. As in the old days, Mostowa Street runs down the slope, extra muros, i.e. in the New and not the Old Town. Though Mostowa was separated from the walls by a swampy moat full of frogs and lizards, the chiming of the bells of the Church of Our Lady reached here in all its glory.

New Town Market Square changed over the centuries. Its current look was determined, to a large extent, by the construction of the church and convent of the Sisters of the Holy Sacrament in 1688–1692, founded by Queen Marysieńka Sobieski and designed by the architect Tylman van Gameren. The convent behind its grated windows survived, and has remained in isolation until today. Only in the days of the Warsaw Uprising in 1944 were the sisters torn from profound contemplation and forced to go out into the open daylight, when the church and the convent became an asylum for the wounded and fugitives.

After the Uprising, the New Town lay, once again, in ruins. Roughly eighty percent of it had been destroyed. And once again it was rebuilt, to become – as some might say –

more beautiful than ever, with the Sisters of the Holy Sacrament's Church and, nestled behind it, the Church of St. Benon, which housed a knife factory before the Second World War. The asymmetrical and sligthly sloping market square came back to life, and the good spirits may well have returned to guard it against any further dangers. Around here, on the south side, over the cinema or next to it, lived the world-famous poet and writer of satyrical verse, Stanisław Jerzy Lec, who wrote: "How can you tell a historic thunderstorm? – It attacks your bones for a long time afterwards".

Before we enter the medieval, and yet quite young, Barbican and cross the boundaries of the Old Town, let us take one last look behind us. One can almost hear the rustle of the Mazovian forests from afar, the roar of bison and elks, the voices of hunters and bee-keepers. The shadow of the brick belfry of the Church of Our Lady gives life another, seemingly slower rhythm...

The Church of the Holy Sacrament on New Town Market Square

History gradually moved southward (let us ignore the few retreats it made). It hesitated for several hundred years and then rushed southward again towards far-away Kraków. To cross the round brick bastion of the Barbican fortifications (inventively recreated before and after the Second World War) onto Nowomiejska (New Town) Street is to move from one municipality, one chapter of history, to another. At the same time, it is a step back into Old Town territory, a small area in which history has stormed the longest.

So much has happened around Market Square, a rectangular, seventy-three-by-ninety-metre open space, that it is mind-blowing!

The city annalist Franciszek Sobieszczański wrote:

"Who ever pays the slightest attention to the area in Warsaw called the Old Town, nowadays? Who, apart from housewives, knows the market square there? Naturally, at the sight of the market square's entire expanse tightly packed with meat stalls and vendors, anyone would want to get away as fast as possible from the air hemmed in by houses and escape from the hustle and bustle of traders and customers".

The Barbican

It is true that the air here is the same as it was 130 odd years ago, when it was "hemmed in by houses", but where are the stalls and stands? Everything has changed. – The ups and downs of history swept away that market and reincarnated it later, pouring new contents into its old shell.

Back to Sobieszczański for just a moment:

"And what will you say, dear readers, if I assure you that this inconspicuous Old Town Market Square was Warsaw's original core, and was for many years its centre of activity, a place in which all local social, industrial, and commercial establishments originated (...) In addition, the market square is Warsaw's forum and was also home to the dukes of Mazovia and the city's wealthiest residents".

And what is more: the market square in old Warsaw has been the scene of so many events, that it is enough to make one positively dizzy. Events of great importance to the state have taken place here, bloody battles were fought here, and public executions were performed. Unfortunately, there was no sound recording equipment around at the time to capture the rowdy singing of guests leaving the cellars beneath what used

to be the town hall, nor the crazed screams of Michał Piekarski, who was tortured in a horrific way for his part in the attempted murder of King Zygmunt III Vasa ("to moan like Piekarski on the rack", as the old Polish saying goes). There are no recordings of the famous 16th-century sermons of father Piotr Skarga, the merry welcoming cries in honour of the victorious commander and national hero, Stefan Żółkiewski, nor of the bells and trumpets warning residents about the outbreak of an epidemic, the howling gale that tore down the tower of St. John's Cathedral in 1606, or the loud uproar when, in 1607, three quarters of the houses on the market square perished in flames from bonfires lit by servants

Old Town **Market** Square

of the nobility. Silent is the echo of protests of the Black Procession, which was formed here on 2 December 1788 and marched down the streets, demanding that the Sejm and the king grant full civic rights to the townspeople. Long gone are the noises coming from Castle Square, when a march was held there in honour of the Decembrists of 1831, or shots and explosions during wars against the Swedes, and then Kościuszko's national insurrection (1794), the January insurrection (1863) and the Warsaw Uprising (1944)...

Several dozen more events could be added to the list. Standing on Market Square in the evening, one is less excited by all the cultural treasures around than by the complex thriller that has gon on for hundreds of years.

Strange have been the fates of some of the houses and prominent personalities. The mind rushes right back to the night of 8 May 1794 when three men, distinguished members of the community, where hanged here as contemptible traitors to the fatherland. Now we imagine swarms of people around the closely packed stalls on Old Town Market Square, followed by a large political demonstration: Emperor Napoleon and Prince Józef Poniatowski, the commander-in-chief of the Polish Army, proceed along double rows of French and Polish soldiers... Or: a downtrodden man in an iron cage in which dishonest bakers, butchers, and vendors were locked up...

The tradition of trade (it has survived until today, although now it mostly involves works of art and "art") was perhaps most strongly associated with the market. Over entire centuries, the well-stocked shops and storerooms of the Old Town Market attracted all kinds of thieves and criminals and required constant vigilance and the mobilisation of defense forces. The lives and property of citizens were protected with varying success – also against outside attacks – by a double ring of walls, a deep moat, drawbridges, a dozen or so watchtowers, and four double gates that were shut tight for the night. The fortifications waned, as the robbery business as well as the war business became more sophisticated. In the years of insurgent battles led at the end of the 18th century by General Tadeusz Kościuszko, who is famous both in Poland and in the United States, and also by the ingenious cobbler Jan Kiliński, there was no longer any fortress. Only for a short time in the heated days of August 1944, did visions of a closed and fortified city under siege revive, followed by the destruction of the entire area and the death of thousands of people fighting to defend it.

Some tourist guides claim that the authenticity of this area vanished into thin air and rose up into the sky along with the smoke and ashes of the dead city. The victors of Warsaw Uprising proved what barbarians they really were, by finishing off casualties with cold premeditation, and by burning down the walls of houses. After the bloodiest battle in the Second World War, a deadly silence prevailed here.

After the war came "the wonder it the Old Town". The reconstruction or, rather, the construction of old Warsaw from scratch, was made possible thanks to ingenious engineering and architecture, as well as the fierce determination of the entire nation to resuscitate this murdered district. The success was phenomenal, although critics maliciously refer to "the wonderful, monumental model town".

Warsaw's Forum Romanum is just the Old Town Market Square and the eight little streets that grow out of it, one of them being Kamienne Schodki (Stone Steps) – a flight of stairs between the blocks, leading down toward the Vistula. The market square is surrounded by town houses, of which only one survived in its original state (that of the dukes of Mazovia), while another, Pod Murzynkiem ("The Black Boy") was saved up to the first floor – the rest, however, were but a tragic pile of rubble.

The Market Square's four "sides of the world" are: the Dekert side to the north, the Barss side to the east, the Zakrzewski side to the south and the Kołłątaj side to the west. The north side is taken up by the Warsaw Historical Museum, where one can watch a short but shattering documentary film about the annihilation and reconstruction of the city. The east side includes the Adam Mickiewicz Museum of Literature. Worthy of attention on the south side of the square is the restaurant "Bazyliszek", while on the western side, you can stop off for a short break at the Fukier wine cellar.

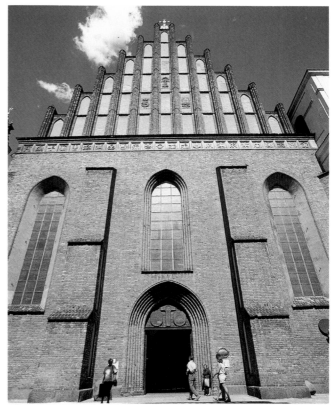

Front of St. John's Cathedral

It is hard to believe that, for centuries, the short and narrow street linking Market Square and Castle Square, Świętojańska, fulfilled the role of the city's main throroughfare. Like city, like main street. There are thirty-eight houses standing on Świętojańska, exactly as they did three hundred years ago. In the neighbourhood of the parish church, today's St. John's Cathedral, the first big city shops and cafes were opened: one of the oldest bookshops (17th century), the first printing house, the renowned Gugenmus watch-maker's, Stanisław Gautier's famous woollens store, and Zygmunt Plocer's pastry shop. On the subject of this small but unusually important street, the poet and annalist of Old Warsaw, Wiktor Gomulicki, wrote: "...Every day, the street bubbled over with activity and noise... Along here, townspeople, summoned by the townhall bell, hurried along to attend a session of the municipal council; citizens entering the city through the Kraków Gate proceeded down this street, while jurists led their clients to the opulent cellars underneath the town hall; it is along here that carts loaded with goods brought in from around the world for customers in the Old Town trundled along, and that the gilded carriages of the nobility drifted past; finally, it is here that bishops, canons, and ordained as well as non-ordained priests wondered around in black and purple garments, students in semisecular gowns and beggars in navy blue cloaks marked with a red cross".

In fact, tiny Świętojańska never lost its high status. The existence of this street alone explains why so-called Varsovia antiqua has been restored to the city and the country. The whole reconstructed, historical urban complex rests upon the backbone of Świętojańska.

Lavishly gilded carriages no longer drive down the short and narrow street between Market Square and Castle Square (a shame indeed!), but people in red and purple can still be seen walking around. When the weather is good, especially on holidays and weekends, this old canyon of a street fills up to the brim with crowds. All visitors to Warsaw, both native and foreign, must pass this joyful and colourful way. A certain disharmony is introduced by modern-version individuals in navy-blue capes with red crosses on their backs – now beggars are less uniform in appearance and are on the whole younger in age, often with AIDS signs displayed on their outstretched legs or their chests.

Świętojańska Street offers a fair number of art and architectural treasures, that were preserved or brought back to life after the war. Nowhere else in the city is the clicking sound of camera shutters so frequent as in and around St. John's Cathedral and the neighbouring Jesuit Church. Through the narrow opening on Piwna Street one can see the tower of St. Martin's Church on the one hand, and on the other, Dziekania Street which runs down the Cathedral's length. That moment when bells of all the places of worship in the Old Town ring in unison is quite special. Once upon a time, the sound of a musical ensemble would resound until late at night from the belfry of St. Martin's. A miraculously preserved mood of ancient mysticism is full of symbols of days barely gone by – those of awesome sacrifice and suffering on the part of thousands who defended the Old Town during the 1944 Uprising. The Cathedral, and this should be remembered, is probably the only great sanctuary in the world, to have housed the front line for so many days and to have been the scene of frequent battles fought with the use of heavy artillery and tanks; in the wall of the Cathedral on the Dziekania side, one now sees a large fragment of caterpillar track from a Goliath mine-tank, which, on exploding, killed many people and blew up a part of the Cathedral.

St. Martin's Church on Piwna Street

Historical cataclysms are over, and the Cathedral is once again, "as good as new". A little different than before the War, and "better" in terms of style; its pre-war English Gothic style was abandoned, and its earlier look was restored. So much has happened in the past that the present-day basilica can only be seen as a partial reconstruction – "the rest is silence".

But first things first. The full name of the shrine is Basilica of the Decapitation of St. John the Baptist. It is most probable that a wooden church stood here as early as the 14th century. Prince Janusz I the Elder had it rebuilt in brick. In 1406, it was proclaimed the parish church, then a collegiate church, and finally (1793) a cathedral and (1960) a basilica. Thus, it has, for centuries now, been the most important place of worship in the city.

From the end of the 16th century, the Cathedral was linked to the Castle by a hidden passage way. A tower was erected but subsequently collapsed. There was a fire, reconstruction, transformation, reconstruction yet again... A series of catastrophes and tragedies – coupled with a fierce determination to keep the place alive.

All the objects and elements in the Cathedral's interior have suffered martyrdom. Perhaps the most valuable is the wonderful tombstone of the last dukes of Mazovia, Stanisław and Janusz. It was created in the early 16th century by Bernardino de Gianotis and Jan Cini, while its foundress was Anne, Duchess of Mazovia; it was later placed over the coffins with the corresponding inscriptions. There are many myths associated with the lives and deaths of the last rulers of independent Mazovia, including one claiming that they died of poisoning.

Inside the basilica is the reconstructed monument to the Speaker of the Four-Year Sejm, Stanisław Małachowski, designed by Bertel Thorvaldsen and carved by F. Max Labourer. There are also numerous tombstones and epitaphs, that also have started a "new life". The Baroque stalls founded by King Jan III as well as the baptismal font from 1632 are reconstructions. The Chapel of the Literary Confraternity (15th century) was rebuilt from scratch, and the Baryczko Chapel, the Chapel of the Miraculous Lord Jesus, the Chapel of the Flagellation, and that of the Holy Sacrament were all restored.

In the old crypts of the basilica are the tombs of President Gabriel Narutowicz, Cardinal August Hlond, Henryk Sienkiewicz, Cardinal Stefan Wyszyński, as well as those of Janusz I the Elder, Bolesław III, the dukes of Mazovia, Stanisław and Janusz, as well as that of Izabela of Vasa.

To complete our story about the Cathedral and the present-day basilica: the verdict over Poland's dispute against Teutonic Knights over Pomerania (1339) was announced in this church. It is also here that the coronations of Kings Stanisław Leszczyński and Stanisław August Poniatowski took place and that the 3rd of May Constitution was sworn in as one of the first progressive basic laws in the world. Under the Communist regime, patriotic demonstrations were organised here during the Martial Law period.

The Tomb of the last dukes of Mazovia: Stanisław (1501–1524) and Janusz (1502–1526)

All Warsaw chroniclers have written about the Cathedral and Świętojańska Street. Sobieszczański maintained: "Within the former limits of the fortified walls the first place was taken up by today's Street of Saint John. Prominent in many ways, it was one of the streets leading off the entrance to the Old Town from Krakowskie Przedmieście..." In his conclusion, Sobieszczański praises the town house Pod Okrętem ("The Ship"), whose owners had been running a flourishing trade with Venice and the East since the days of King Władysław IV. Later on, "the wine business there kept going for a long time, and was much frequented and very popular throughout the country."

Before leaving the Old Town, one ought to make a couple of detours from the main route and explore the side streets. For example, one can turn into Dziekania Street and take a look at the Cathedral from behind and at Kanonia, where until two hundred years ago, a cemetery still existed. Houses were put up here as early as the 15th century. These were then burned down, then rebuilt, just as the rest of the Old Town. This enchantingly irregular street, or square, was paved about the time when the cemetery disappeared, which, at the time, caused quite a sensation. The old Rococo figure of Our Lady has survived all these years.

Many poets, including Wiktor Gomulicki and Or-Ot, chose to live behind the Cathedral. This is where the first seat of the Warsaw Scientific Society was located.

Kanonia has its own rich history, worthy of a novel or a film script. The windows that looked eastward onto the Vistula belonged to canons and prelates, noblemen, proudly displaying their coats of arms over their doorways, distinguished townspeople – the Rzeszek, Chawłosz, and Giz families... For a long time, there was a dark prison cell somewhere along here, later – which may sound somewhat macabre – transformed into a morgue whose clientele was made up predominantly of people who had drowned in the Vistula.

Kanonia Street

With the flow of the centuries, names in the Old Town changed. Piwna (Brewery) Street, which runs parallel to Świętojańska, was previously called Szynkarska (Inn) Street and Marcinkańska (Martin) Street. Here, Warsaw's first hospital, named after the Holy Spirit, and a shelter for the poor were set up. Many prominent figures used to live in this narrow street including Royal Court's physician Wojciech Oczko and another physician, meteorologist, historian, and author of *Warsaw Aesthetics,* Antoni Magier (both now have streets named after them in Warsaw). At No. 6, Halina Kosmólska-Szulc lived after the War-caretaker of Old Town's pigeons, present in films and photographs from the period of post-War reconstruction.

And naturally, there is the Augustinian church and monastery, the popular Saint Martin's, founded in 1356 by the Mazovian ruler at the time. Although remodelled on several occasions, it has retained its pantina of antiquity. The interior was modernised after wartime destruction and is the subject of general admiration; it was designed by the Franciscan nun and architect, Alma Skrzydlewska. St. Martin's Church played a major role during Martial Law in 1981–82 and later on; it is here that action to help victims of the regime was concentrated, and it was the site of dramatic scenes during "forays" by the militia and security forces.

Scraps of historical documents have been miraculously preserved – the dents in a burnt-down crucifix were replenished with metal in a skillful way, the remains of Baroque and Gothic details were saved. There is the tomb of Adam Jarzębski, Warsaw's first annalist, in the crypt. On the lateral pillars of the church are plaques commemorating members of the Parachute Brigade of the Polish Armed Forces in Great Britain, and girl scouts who died in the Second World War. The gate through the tower leads on to a courtyard surrounded by arcades.

Any guide would be tempted to sidetrack from the main route, for example to walk along Piekarska Street to Podwale where the monument to the heroic cobbler, Jan Kiliński, stands. Along Podwale, a stretch of old city walls has been recreated. Almost

Castle Square

right behind Kiliński's back stands an 18th-century building which now houses the Museum of Arts and Crafts and Precision Industries, attracting one's attention by a clock that chimes. The tiny little square in front of this house was once a place for public executions (people were burnt alive at the stake). For this reason, local residents called it "Little Hell".

Podwale leads back towards the New Town, where there are still quite a few sights to visit. The monument to the tragic explosion of a booby-trap mine on Kiliński Street in 1944, the Dominican church on Freta (preaching Holy Mass in Latin), the house where Maria Skłodowska-Curie was born... But let us return to the main route.

For centuries, history focused upon the Old and New Towns, later however it ran wild beyond the walls and the crowded couryards. Life poured over the Old Town's boundaries into Castle Square.

For several hundred years, across the area above the steep terraces of the Vistula escarpment (thirty five metres over the shining waters of the river!), a road led southwards – via the city of Jazdów to Czersk and beyond. Then, apparently in the late 14th century, the Townspeople's Gate, later renamed "Kraków Gate", was erected on today's Senatorska Street.

However, Krakowskie Przedmieście did not yet exist at the time. The road leading that way was, according to certain scholars, also called Freta (in medieval Latin: uncultivated field – the street running out from the Old Town towards the north now bears the same name). Maybe Freta did exist, maybe not – one thing for certain is that an artery by the name of Czerskie Przedmieście (Czersk Suburb) did at some point exist. Some historians quote more names: Przedmieście Bernardyńskie, Rynek Bernardyński, Rynek Przedmiejski. Krakowskie Przedmieście was born in the year 1580 and must have been, at the time, a "third-class road with a non-hardened surface".

And where is Castle Square? And where is the Castle?

It is hard to believe this, but Castle Square was, between the 15th and 16th centuries but a yard, that is to say a vast castle forecourt, and was therefore, to all intents and purposes, nonexistent. It did not go up in status until 1644 when King Zygmunt's Column was to be erected in front of Kraków Gate. Twelve years later, during the Swedish invasion, the grounds were transformed into a bastion and were narrowed down rather than expanded. It is not until the early 19th century that a project for a radical transformation of the area around the Castle and its inclusion within the urban layout of the city, was carried out. A great deal was demolished. The Kraków Gate was dismantled, the square was given the shape of an irregular triangle. In 1843, the Bernardine St. Clare Sisters' Convent neighbouring upon the Castle was taken apart, many houses were pulled down. It is only then that this beautiful square, so incredibly vital to the capital city, came into being.

Designs for the configuration of Castle Square were elaborated under the rule of the last king of Poland by the outstanding architects: Victor Louis, Efraim Schroeger, Jakub Fontana, and Domenico Merlini. Not all the excellent designs were carried out, but they certainly influenced further changes, and, above all, shaped the opening of the square onto Krakowskie Przedmieście.

Before the square took on its current form, major events were already taking place there. In the years 1656 and 1704, it served as a regular battlefield with the Swedes. Later, during the Kościuszko Insurrection, the first in a series of national rebellions, more storms followed. During long years of Partitions, here, "before King Zygmunt's very eyes", Cossacks charged upon the assembled population of Warsaw. Finally, the square filled up with the roar of guns during the 1944 Uprising.

Monument to King Zygmunt III Vasa

The monarch – one of Warsaw's symbolic landmarks – crashed down from his column onto the paving stones. Shortly afterwards, when the first residents of the city returned to this square littered with rubble, they had the rare opportunity to see, close-up, the bronze face of the king. Soon, people lifted Zygmunt up, like nurses might have lifted a patient onto a stretcher, and moved him to St. Anne's Church, and then to the luckily saved building of the National Museum, where he became one of the exhibits in the famous exhibition "Warsaw Accuses".

The restored monument stood on the square once again in 1949, and the king took up his observation post at the very top of the column, to watch over the somewhat altered landscape of the city – Śląsko-Dąbrowski Bridge, the district of Mariensztat, the first reconstructed buildings along King's Road.

The statue of Zygmunt III Vasa, the oldest secular monument in Warsaw and one of the first such in Europe, is the work of the architect Constantino Tencalla and the sculptor Clemente Molli. By some sheer coincidence, exactly three hundred years elapsed between the day the statue was placed on the column in 1644, at the instance of King Zygmunt's son Władysław IV, and the day it fell to the ground in 1944, shattered to pieces by a German missile.

Despite the column's significance, Castle Square is dominated by the Royal Castle. During the Second World War, first in September 1939, and then at the end of 1944, the enemy did everything they could to obliterate Warsaw's Castle, the prime symbol of continuity in Polish history. First bombed and burned down, and then blown up – the appearance of this section of the city had been altered for decades to come. Until the 1970's, when it was rebuilt almost from scratch, the traditional skyline of Warsaw from the river had a large dent in it.

Similarly to the Cathedral and many palaces, the Castle was initially made of wood, and only considerably later was it built of brick. Although the exact date is impossible to determine, it is in the 13th century that the dukes of Mazovia built a residence here. Next to it, flowed the brook Kamionka and a settlement, and later a town, took shape. In the first half of the 14th century, on the Vistula escarpment, the Great Tower, i.e. the City Tower, a link in city walls, was erected. At first, in the early 15th century, a brick Great

The Royal Castle

Manor House neighboured upon the Great Tower; this was the residence of the Duke of Mazovia Janusz I; a building on three levels, fifteen by fourty-eight metres in size. Throughout the 15th century, it was was extended and new buildings were added.

The story borders on a myth... The Castle retained its original form up to Mazovia's annexation by the Polish Kingdom. It is not until 1570 that King Zygmunt August began to transform his Warsaw residence, changing its style from Gothic to Renaissance; and employing Italian masters, such as Giovanni Battista Quardo and Jacopo Parr. Nevertheless, it is King Zygmunt III who commissioned work for the Castle's complete transformation when Poland's capital was moved from Kraków to Warsaw. Again, Italian masters, such as Jacopo Rodondo, Mateusz Castelli, and Giovanni Trevano, worked on the five-winged shell of the building at the turn of the 16th and 17th centuries. It is then that the three-level wings originated: the north, west, and south wings with the City, Noblemen's, and Senator's Gates. Over the Noblemen's Gate, a sixty-metre tower was erected and topped with a high dome. A clock was added to the tower in 1622. It is this tower, the Zygmunt or Clock Tower, that imprinted itself in the memory of Warsaw residents in September 1939. Many still retain before their eyes the vision of the burning tower and the motionless hands of the clock...

Thus, Warsaw and the Polish nation have the monarchs of the Vasa Dynasty to thank for the Royal Castle, now a permanent feature of the city landscape. Although the structure is basically Italian Baroque in style, one's attention is almost inevitably drawn by its similarity to the Vasa Family's castle on the Swedish island of Oland. It may be pure coincidence, but perhaps it was the wish of the Castle's royal patrons?

Later, when Warsaw's Castle became the seat of power in the state and the main administrative offices of the Republic were housed there, the secret passage linking the Castle with the parish church was completed. This was accomplished after Michał Piekarski's attempt on the king's life, when the latter was on his way to the church to pray.

The Vasa's masterpiece was completed by Władysław, son of Zygmunt. Court Theatre Hall was built. The Władysław Tower was remodelled in Baroque style with a staircase (designed by Tencalla). But it is the interior that was embellished the most.

In 1655, a Swedish invasion caused a ruthless destruction of Warsaw. Among other things, the Castle fell prey to the invaders, even though it had been the residence of descendants of a Swedish royal family. However, there was no love lost between the Swedes from Sweden and their former compatriots, expecially since the Polish monarchs had laid claim to the throne in Stockholm and used the title of King of Sweden, which must have greatly irritated their cousins on the other of side the Baltic.

The interiors of the Castle were destroyed. All of the most valuable pieces of furniture and works of art were pillaged and taken out of Poland to Sweden (where they may be seen to this very day).

The Castle was now dreary, and successive kings moved to other palaces. Slowly, the Castle rooms were redecorated. But then the Swedes returned to Warsaw and devastated the place once more. The Saxons restored part of it later on. Under August III, the Baroque elevation facing the Vistula was erected (Gaetano Chiaveri, Antonio Solari). At the same time, the Senate Chamber was moved to the first floor, one of the royal rooms was turned into the Throne Room. Further innovations followed later on: at the foot of the slope, the Great Annex was built on two levels, and the Castle was given a new façade on the Vistula side.

Finally, the place became the property of an exceptionally generous lord and patron – Stanisław August Poniatowski. In 1774–1777, the chief royal architect, Domenico Merlini was commissioned to redesign many of the Royal Castle's rooms. The Castle's magnificent interiors were created by Jacopo Fontana, Victor Louis, Domenico Merlini, and Jan Chrystian Kamsetzer.

In the 1990s, the Castle is back on city maps. Keen fans, artists and craftsmen sealed that painful gap in Warsaw's skyline in 1976, and the "old", "historic" object is back there in its old place. In one hundred years' time, few will be aware that for several decades Warsaw was deprived of its Castle.

Many objects and works of art from the Castle interiors, survived, many, such as the frescos of Bacciarelli (including the one-hundred-and-fifty-square-metre ceiling in the Ballroom), will never be seen again. Among the treasures regained are 300 paintings, 70 sculptures, 15 fireplaces, and lots of furniture. Details made it possible to recreate some to the wood panelling, parquet floors, and stucco work. A stream of gifts flowed in from around the country and abroad.

Today, thousands of people enter via the marble stairs, and step into the Throne Hall, the Knight's Room, the Ballroom, the Dining Hall, the Royal Chapel, King Stanisław's Study and about one hundred other wonderful interiors. The residence of the Polish kings and of the last president of pre-War Poland hosts state ceremonies, although it is now also open to the general public. Yet another miracle on the Vistula!

Many accounts like this one have been written in the past, starting with Adam Jarzębski's: "And now the Castle I shall portray, I remember it well, a frail array / No walls of brick, just wood so thick (...) Now we have one built anew / straight to the point, without to-do / bricks from abroad for a structure so fair, / built at great cost, no expense to spare".

Jarzębski remembered the wooden Castle and praised its new, brick form (although experts on the subject criticise him, pointing out that the original structure was already partly built of brick). We, however, remember ruins and wastelands, and cherish the building that is perfectly "true to life".

On the East-West Highway (Trasa W-Z) side of the Castle, as if blending in with it, is Pałac Pod Blachą (Tin-Roofed Palace, 1720), the property of King Stanisław August, and later that of Prince Józef Poniatowski, now the office of Warsaw's chief architect.

Archeologist alone benefit from destruction and turmoil. On Castle Square, they nexcavated under the paving stones and the asphalt an old, Gothic bridge, remnants of the town house of King Zygmunt August's physician and alchemist, Baltazar Smosarski, English china dishes, and various other amazing items.

We must mention the tunnel built after the second World War under Miodowa Street and Castle Square, i.e. that of the East-West Highway, a thoroughfare linking the districts of Wola and Praga: this was a bold idea of town planners and architects, supported by thousands of workers.

Now, we enter Krakowskie Przedmieście — the favourite street of Warsaw residents. We already know how the Old Town and the Royal Castle were reincarnated — what happened on this section of King's Road belongs to the same category of "life after life".

The Throne Hall at the Royal Castle

The East-West Highway

The street's modern history is without precedent in the world. The architects and conservationists who recreated destroyed and lost treasures of art, especially those on Krakowskie Przedmieście, were asisted by... Bernardo Belotto, known as a "Canaletto junior", an artist born in 1726 in Venice. To be more precise: contemporary builders relied on of canvases by the great urban landscape artist, who carefully recorded the way Warsaw looked in the second half of the 18th century. These were sometimes the only documents they had to base their work on, since a large proportion of maps, drawings, and photographs had been ruined irreversibly.

By sheer luck, and the resourcefulness of certain people, twenty five pictures were saved and returned to the capital after having been repeatedly stolen, removed, and thereatened with fire.

Warsaw Panorama
(Canaletto, 1770)

Master Canaletto recorded the most important objects, depicted the main arteries, and even described street scenes. Works of art, but also – as we might now say – a reporter's observations. Hence the enormous documentary value of landscapes by the Italian artist, who recorded the cityscape with unremitting precision; besides, we know that he used the dark chamber (camera obscura) in his work.

Famous is Canaletto's painting depicting Castle Square opening on Krakowskie Przedmieście. If it were not for the masses of cars and other modern accessories, the view we now have of John's House at the corner and the street itself would fit in pretty closely with the Italian painter's visions. Just this attic roof, the intricate Rococo façade, the gutters (gargoyles) in the form of dragons. This house and the neighbouring one have been home to writers for a dozen-odd years. On the ground floor area facing the square, escalators have been installed (they are often out of order). Under the Duchy of Warsaw, the young and the old used to gather near the Zygmunt Column in the hope of finding work (they were known at the time as the "Zygmunt loafers"). Today, one comes across loafers by the top of the escalators, although few of them are looking for work.

From under the foot of the Column, one has a full view over (if there are no cars blocking the view) the perspective of Krakowskie Przedmieście. Even on a weekday, there is something very grand about this view. The wide, irregular street lined with uneven rows of houses is filled with light, even on a cloudy day. This is where lovers, pensioners, tourists, and others for that matter, most like to stroll. Someone suggested that the pavements on Krakowskie Przedmieście and Nowy Świat be covered, so that one should be able to go for a walk in all kinds of weather.

Today this is the favourite street among Varsavians. However, it does happen – as has always been the case – that history has made its way down here, too. How many times joyful, sad, rebellious, laughing, weeping, and fighting crowds flowed along this street. Just as Edinburgh has its famous Royal Mile, Warsaw has its one-kilometre-long King's Road – which is, in fact, the most important kilometre in Poland.

We already know what went on in Castle Square over the centuries – with the flow of time, events boiled over into Krakowskie Przedmieście. In front of the Bernardine Church of St. Anne's, Prussian princes paid homage to the Polish kings and battles were fought with the Swedes. It is right here that mass anti-Russian demonstrations were held in the 1860s and bloody pacification measures were implemented. Right by St. Anne's Church, the Pope, John Paul II, made a speech and was greeted by hundreds of thousands of people. This is commemorated in a plaque placed in front of the shrine.

The Church of St. Anne erected in 1454 also had an eventful past. It too was demolished and rebuilt several times – a cycle that seems so normal in this city that one ceases to be surprised by it. The academic church we see today, with its classical façade (by Chrystian Aigner and Stanisław Kostka-Potocki), its early-Gothic presbytery and its historic confessionals, survived an additional and exceptional tragedy: After its reconstruction in 1949, it began to slide down the slope, but was saved by applying a special method of consolidating the slope with stone.

The first section of Krakowskie Przedmieście, previously Bernardyński Square, from Castle Square to the entrance of Miodowa Street and the fork with the green area (called Hoover Gardens before the War), was the city's first step towards a modern future. Many years later, someone wrote: "This street is akin to the recess of a door in which the height of a growing child is marked. It is a measure of the city's development, and an illustrated record of its history".

The child has been growing long enough. Jan Stanisław Bystroń, a distinguished authority on Warsaw, reminds us of the city's long and hard childhood. Back in 1814, the Russian chief of department for Warsaw wrote to the head of the police force: "A considerable amount of mud on the streets has got so bad that, not only do local residents and the military feel ill at ease, but even vehicles face serious difficulties and drive up there at great risk". About the same time Krakowskie Przedmieście, and neighbouring Miodowa and Senatorska Streets were lit by square lanterns hung up on lines between two posts.

Bystroń noted that in 1819 there were 245 such lanterns. Besides, linkmen offered their services to guide people along the dark streets. From dusk till dawn, safety was ensured by the so-called patrollers (thirty at first, later sixty), who did their rounds, equipped with halberds and clappers.

So it was until last century, which was practically yesterday! Of course, the further back one goes, the worse its was – trash used to be thrown onto the street where it rotted and poisoned the air. The streets were neither paved nor lit. Today, such cities can be seen in the depths of Africa or in the darkest corners of Asia.

Therefore, it is worth remembering about the aforementioned "racess in a door", when walking down Warsaw's showcase, Krakowskie Przedmieście.

Many things, good and bad, have gone forever – yet some evidence of continuity survived. And so, in a square that was once built up, a figure of Our Lady of Passau still stands. It was created by Józef Bellotti (1683), in thanksgiving for the salvation of the city from the plague and for the victory in Vienna. The triumphal gate in honour of King Jan III Sobieski, who defeated the Turks, has disappeared; it stood crosswise to the street, opposite St. Anne's Church, and the cost of its construction exceeded Warsaw's then entire annual budget!

St. Anne's Church

To add some gossip to history, in one of the houses that had stood here lived the fortune-teller, Mme Henrietta Zofia Lhullier, who apparently predicted that Stanisław August Poniatowski would ascend the throne when he himself had no reason to expect this yet. The beautiful Mrs. Elżbieta Grabowska, the secret great love of Poland's last king, also had an apartment here.

Nearly all the houses now standing on this street (put up there to replace wooden houses and palaces) lay in ruins in 1945. They were rebuilt from scratch, using all the elements of the façades saved from the Nazis. The Civic Club returned to life. Once the place of loud entertainment and mascarades, it is now the headquarters Polish émigré organisation, the "Polish Community". At the corner of Bednarska, a picturesque street sloping down towards the Vistula, the Warsaw Philanthropic Society, an institution founded at the beginning of the last century, is back in operation. Next comes Dziekanka, the former seat of the dean of the Warsaw chapter, later on an inn, and now a female students' boarding house. We now approach the Carmelite Church with its 18th century interior and façade; here, in 1656, from the terrace adjoining the cloister Maria Ludwika ordered to fire canons at the Swedish army storming Warsaw. The top of the façade designed by Schroeger is decorated by a copper sphere with a serpent wrapped round it and pressed down by a chalice with the host – this sphere gave rise to the local saying "to swell up like a carmelite balloon".

Opposite the Carmelite Church, on a little square at the corner of Trębacka Street, is former Saxon Post (until 1878), now the Attorney General's office, less attractive to strollers than the neighbouring and ever lively café – previously called "Telimena" and now called "Galeria M" – at the corner of Krakowskie Przedmieście and Kozia Street. For some time in the 19th century, on the first floor of the building now housing the Attorney General's office, the Mach Brothers ran a waxworks studio and the little Theatre of Magic Tricks.

In the middle of the road, between the Carmelite Church and the Saxon Post, stands the monument to Adam Mickiewicz, sculpted by Cyprian Godebski and unveiled in 1898 – during the Partition period. The ceremony turned into a great anti-Tsarist demonstration, and Stanisław Moniuszko's *Prayer* was played for the occasion. No speeches were made – the authorities did not allow writer Henryk Sienkiewicz to address the crowd.

Many more demonstrations were held near the bronze monument of the Poet, both in 1905, and under the communist regime.

The statue is tremendous (four-and-a-half metres high) and extremely impressive. Equally wonderful is the hand-forged wrought iron fence around the monument – a gift from the Zieleziński Works.

We proceed down the mere few hundred metres of major history the charming avenue that links the Castle and the Palace of Stanisław Staszic. It is but a link in a great chain – that of King's Road – but the significance and charm of this particular section of the route never fail to attract people's attention. Be it newcomers from outside or residents of the city proper.

Further on from the Mickiewicz Monument and the Carmelite Church, Krakowskie Przedmieście narrows down, mainly because of the Radziwiłł Palace, and then Hotel

Monument to Adam Mickiewicz

Bristol. From here on, everything on this street is palatial in appearance and richly ornamented with monuments.

After Mickiewicz, there's a monument of featuring Prince Józef Poniatowski on a horse, then, pretty shamefully hidden in the bushes, that of local writer Bolesław Prus. Further along, in front of the Church of the Visitation Nuns, stands the monument to the Primate Stefan Wyszyński. Finally, at the point where Krakowskie Przedmieście becomes Nowy Świat, stands the monument to Mikołaj Kopernik. A choice company indeed.

Here we have two truly magnificent palaces: the Radziwiłł Palace to the left, at No. 46/48, and the Potocki Palace to the right, at No. 15. Today, the former belongs to the Council of Ministers, while the latter serves as the headquarters of the Ministry of Culture and Art.

Their very names involve a whole story all to themselves. The Radziwiłł Palace was commissioned back in 1643 by the royal hetman, Stanisław Koniecpolski, and was designed by Constantino Tencalla. Later on, the palace belonged to the Lubomirski family, and finally to the Radziwiłł family. The name Radziwiłł has stuck.

Sometimes the place is referred to as the Russian Governor's Palace because, in 1818, it became the residence of the Governor-general of the Congress Kingdom.

It was not until the mid-18th century that the palace acquired its lateral wings, those protruding out towards the street. They were designed by yet another Italian architect, Antonio Solari. Later, the oustanding architect Chrystian Aigner redesigned it in classical style. In 1820, Camillo Landini added four stone lions to guard the palace. According to a popular local anegdote, they will roar the minute a virtuous Varsavienne walks past.

Before the last war, the Council of Ministers used the building for ceremonial purposes and for receptions. Also after the war, conferences, banquets, the signature of documents (e.g. the signing of the Warsaw Pact in 1955 and the Treaty on the normalisation of relations between Poland and the German Federal Republic in 1970), and ceremonial balls took place here. Earlier, back in 1791, political talks were held here by the group known as the Assembly of Friends of the 3rd of May Government Law headed by Hugo Kołłątaj and Julian Ursyn Niemcewicz.

Within the palace courtyard stands the monument to Prince Józef Poniatowski, a work by the famous Danish sculptor, Bertel Thorvaldsen, who based his artistic design on the statue of Marcus Aurelius on the Capitol in Rome.

Monument to Prince Józef Poniatowski

Similarly to the local people, monuments in Poland have at times had tragic fates. The bronze Prince changed place – and not of his own free will either. Thorvaldsen received the commission in 1815 and made the monument. The November Uprising and the punitive measures following defeat made all former plans null and void. The statue, which had long since been completed, transported to Governor-general Ivan Paskievitch's palace in Homel. Meanwhile, in front of the Radziwiłł Palace a statue of... Paskievitch was placed; promptly pulled down in 1915. When, after the First World War, the bronze Prince returned from exile, he was not placed in the place originally allocated for him on Krakowskie Przedmieście, but in front of the Tomb of the Unknown Soldier, on what was then called Saxon Square (now Piłsudski Square). During the Second World War, the monument to the Marshal of Poland and France was destroyed by the occupation forces. Cast anew from a model kept in Denmark, and offered by the people of Copenhagen, it returned to Warsaw; embarrassed by the gift, the communist authorities hid the monument to Józef Poniatowski "in the bushes", in front of the Orangerie in Łazienki. Finally, after countless appeals and statements in the press, consent was given to move the prince onto Krakowskie Przedmieście.

This calls to mind, once again, Stanisław Jerzy Lec's aphorism: "A monument makes a excellent sundial. Even when it is no longer there, you can easily read the hour that has struck".

Straight opposite the Radziwiłł Palace and the Poniatowski Monument, stands the 17th-century Potocki (Denhoff, Czartoryski, Lubomirski) Palace. The palace was redesigned many times by Fontana and Kamsetzer, and above all by Władysław Marconi. Today, behind two magnificent neo-Baroque gates (with railings by the already familiar Zieleziński) is the office of the minister of culture and art. Destroyed during the Second World War, the building was restored to full splendour in 1949. Just a few words on the history of this place: During the Napoleonic era, Marshall Murat lived in the palace, and in 1807, a ceremonial ball was held here in honour of the French Emperor. Art has been there all the time – in the 1880s, the Society for the Promotion of Fine Arts exhibited for the first time in Warsaw and Poland, the great canvasses of the painter Jan Matejko – *The Battle of Grunwald* and *Teutonic Knights Pay Homage to the King*. In the Guardhouse, a separate little building in the palace courtyard, exhibitions of Polish and foreign artists have been held since the end of the War.

The next couple of buildings on either side of Krakowskie Przedmieście are old hotels – the Bristol and the Europejski. Both were built on the sites of old palaces. The Europejski was completed in 1877, to a design by Henryk Marconi, and was declared the first fully modern hotel in Warsaw, while the Bristol (designed by Władysław Marconi) joined it 25 years later (and was, at the time, owned by the renowned pianist and politician, Ignacy Paderewski).

Celebrations at the Tomb of the Unknown Soldier

The restaurants and cafés in both hotels were famous in the city, the most exclusive in the inter-war period being the very chic and fashionable Café Lourse in the Europejski Hotel.

On the left-hand side, just round the corner of the Bristol, Karowa Street runs down towards the Vistula. For many years, thrilling car races were held along the winds and bends of this street. Krakowskie Przedmieście broadens out again. There is a green square where buildings were blown up during the War.

We are now approaching the so-called Saxon Axis. It was the idea of August II the Saxon to build an artery from the Vistula and far into the west. Warsaw, at the time, had barely twenty thousand inhabitants and it was not too tightly built up.

Old Saxon Axis was obstructed by a line of buildings on Krakowskie Przedmieście that disappeared during the last war. Later, the Saxon Palace (which until 1939 housed the general HQ of the army) stood across the Axis, and under its arcades was the Tomb of the Unknown Soldier – this particular obstacle was partially removed by historical events, since the palace was quite simply blown up. Later, in the Saxon Gardens (Ogród Saski) – the wooden Summer Theatre was built, but it, too, fell prey to the ravages of war. A little further, the Gardens were pierced by Marszałkowska Street, and finally – in front of the covered Mirowska Market and the Lubomirski Palace (which was moved around one hundred degrees – a remarkable feat of engineering) – a monument was put up, dedicated to "the people's power" (it has recently been demolished). In other words, the Saxon Axis has had great difficulty in proceeding and is gradually being edged off the map of the city.

The Saxon Palace on former Saxon Square disappeared for ever, but the Tomb of the Unknown Soldier has survived. The triple arcade, the leftovers of the colonnade of the old palace, has been preserved like an ancient ruin. As a result of war and destruction, the Tomb has taken on a dramatic air.

Under the arcades lies the Unknown Soldier, one of those who gave their lives during the war against the Bolsheviks (1918–1920). A flame burns there and soldiers stand on guard, motionless. Until recently, there were still disputes over the plaques featuring the names of battlefields, where Poles have died; for the Communists, the victims of the 1918–20 war did not count, nor did those at certain extermination camps and certain concentration camps in the Soviet Union. Today, the list of plaques has been complemented, and, once again, they speak out loud.

The Rococo Brühl Palace on Piłsudski Square, once the headquarters of the Ministry of Foreign Affairs was literally levelled to the ground during the War. Built on the opposite side of the square, near Królewska Street, Hotel Victoria is one of several hotels planned for this part of town. Perhaps another will appear on nearby Teatralny Square, where the opera house (Teatr Wielki, or Grand Theatre) stands and where new tourist facilities are planned. Teatr Wielki is the work of Antonio Corazzi and was also rebuilt from the ruins.

Teatr Wielki, a truly grand building, with a monumental colonnade, is a mecca for foreigners – opera and ballet, the main performing arts put on here, do, after all, use an international language.

It seems a shame to go back to the main route without taking a look at the Zachęta building (beyond Hotel Victoria), which, for many years now, has been used as an art exhibition centre – mostly painting and sculpture – and at the nearby circular Lutheran Church of the Holy Trinity (a work by Szymon Zug), whose dome collapsed during the War and was later restored. Apart from religious ceremonies, chamber music and choir singing concerts are often held here.

We may now head back to Krakowskie Przedmieście. The Church of the Visitation Nuns at the top of Królewska Street. One of the favourite shrines among local Varsavians. This church is a charming example of 18th-century Baroque architecture, miraculously saved during the Second World War a happy and rare occurence among the city's historical monuments.

The church's beautiful façade with statues of saints among columns, and Rococo figures of angels, was created by Karol Bay and continued by Efraim Schroeger.

The order of the Visitants was brought to Poland from France in 1654 by Marie-Louise Gonzaga, who married two kings in succession: Władysław IV and, following his death, Jan Kazimierz. The church was renovated in 1661. Later, various transformations were undertaken, mostly with successful results. Restoration work was carried out by Henryk Marconi. In the central altar of the church, one's attention is drawn by the figure of the Lord. Like the pulpit in the shape of a boat, it is the work of Jan Jerzy Plersch. The numerous tombstones and epitaphs of distinguished Poles prove the church's rank.

Fryderyk Chopin used to play the organ in the Church of the Visitation Nuns.

In front of the shrine, on a square to the left, is a statue of the Primate of Poland Stefan Wyszyński, apparently pondering about his life between the palace, the cathedral, and prison, or wondering how come the authorities of the Polish People's Republic – admittedly growing weaker by the hour – agreed in 1987 for a bronze statue of the Cardinal to be placed here... A work of Andrzej Renes.

And, finally, Krakowskie Przedmieście from Królewska Street down to the Copernicus Monument. It is along this section that the University campus is located, while the other side is occupied by the Fine Arts Academy and the Church of the Holy Cross, all clustered around the great astronomer sitting on his pedestal.

Warsaw University. One of the most important places on the city map, a secret and invisible "critical point of the capital". It may well be that this feeling among Warsaw residents is determined by the spirits of tradition that linger here, or perhaps is it the influence of this exceptionally high concentration of beauty embedded in the walls and roofs (not to mention the beauty of girls strolling along here).

Church of the Visitation Nuns

One thing for certain is that Fryderyk Chopin was not indifferent to the beauty of this place. He lived in the palace on the corner of present-day Traugutt Street and after his death his heart was buried in the Church of the Holy Cross next door. We have reasons to believe that this place on Krakowskie Przedmieście also featured highly in the life of the hero of the United States and Poland, Tadeusz Kościuszko, who graduated from the Knights' Academy in the Kazimierzowski Palace, i.e. the main building of today's Warsaw University. It is along here that all the great Polish and foreign kings, presidents, and prime ministers have driven past, as have Church dignitaries headed by the Pope, thousands of ministers, prominent artists, outstanding scholars. This street breathes the spirit of the great and the little who have passed along it.

The University courtyard has always been a happy and lively place. However, exceptions to this rule have occurred (e.g. in March 1968, when demonstrations held by young people, disgusted at the anti-Semitic campaign, ended in a massacre of students who gathered here). Straight opposite the gate, at the end of a gentle slope down the courtyard, the view is rounded off by the massive neo-Renaissance building of the University Library (1891–99, designed by Antoni Jabłoński-Jasieńczyk and Stefan Szyller). The library inherited the collection of the Knights' Academy and suffered great damages in 1939–45. Today it is packed full with three-and-a-half million volumes, and the heads of the University are waging a war, with varying success, for new premises to be provided.

Young couples and students swotting for exams are kept company by the clock that chimes, reproducing the first bars of the song *Gaudeamus igitur* (a gift from Warsaw craftsmen in 1967).

The Main Gate of the University

The history of the University, while four times shorter than that of the Jagiellonian Alma Mater in Kraków, is interesting and eventful. For some time, Warsaw University, which the Tsarist authorities renamed the Central School, was responsible for educating the intellectual elite of the nation, and was a hotbed of patriotism. All national uprisings found active support among professors and students at this school. For its part in the 1830 uprising, the barely fourty-year old university was shut down, and was later revived as the Central School. In the end, it was transformed into a Russian school which kept going until 1915. The most dramatic episode in the history of Warsaw University were the War years and the atrocities of the Nazi occupation; lectures continued in the underground, involving a high level of risk and tremendous losses.

Before the University was created, there was the Knights' Academy – school to the cadet corps of King Stanisław August, attended by Tadeusz Kościuszko and other brave sons of the nation.

It is woth remembering all these facts while taking a look behind the Library into the deep recess of the Kazimierzowski Palace.

The palace itself is tucked away behind the Library and now houses the rector's office and the University administration. It was erected in 1634 at King Władysław's request, and altered twenty six years later for King Jan Kazimierz, who used it as a summer residence. The palace then became the property of Jan III Sobieski and August II the Saxon who turned it into barracks for his army. This building must have been exceptionally valuable, since Stanisław August Poniatowski also joined the long list of its owners.

But let us now leave the University complex and cross over to the opposite side of Krakowskie Przedmieście, to an extremely attractive institution, the Fine Arts Academy. It is housed in yet another palace belonging to the Radziejowski, Sieniawski, Czapski and then the Krasiński and Raczyński families. Let us spare ourselves the details as to who built it and who altered the buildings and their adornments: they were artists of the highest degree.

It all began at the end of the 18th century, under the Four-Year Sejm and the 3rd of May Constitution, when the speaker of the house, Stanisław Małachowski resided here. The next tenant was General Wincenty Krasiński, the father of the great poet, Zygmunt Krasiński, who was born here. The general commanded the Polish light cavalry regiment, part of Emperor Napoleon's troops, i.e. the soldiers from Somosierra. The left annex was home to the Chopin family in 1826.

Once again, as is the case opposite the road, we have a beautiful gate with eagles (mid-18th century), as well as a courtyard, yet considerably smaller and quainter than that of the University. In it stands a copy of the 15th century monument by Andrea Verrocchio – a Venetian condottiere, Bartolomeo Colleoni.

Across Traugutt Street, rises the double-spired 16th century Church of the Holy Cross. The original 16th-century shrine in this place was burned down during the Wars with the Swedes and the new church was built to a design by Józef Bellotti. Almost one hundred years later, Józef and Jakub Fontana, with Joachim Jauch's assistance, added a façade with steeples. Later, sculptures of the apostles, Peter and Paul, were fitted in the recesses, as were the figures of angels. The two characteristic flights of stairs were initially set apart from the façade of the church. In the early 19th century, mid-way along the balustrade, statue of Christ bearing the cross (completed by Andrzej Pruszyński) was placed. This holy figure was – as King Zygmunt – knocked down in 1944; photos have been kept of Christ lying on his back on the street, pointing towards heaven.

The Holy Cross shrine had an eventful past. Here the anniversary of the passing of the 3rd of May Constitution was solemnly celebrated in 1792, here, at the foot of the stairs, battles took place during the Kościuszko Insurrection. The funerals of many prominent Poles were held at the church from Prince Józef Poniatowski to Karol Szymanowski. In 1944, fierce fighting between insurgents and the Germans went on within the church for a long time. From here, civilians were led out as live targets for tanks attacking the barricades put up by the insurgents. In the end, a Goliath mine was flung in the church, destroying many objects of historical value and countless works of art.

And yet, the church has remained until today a treasure trove of objects that are valuable and important to the nation. These include tombstones and epitaphs. Walled into the recesses are urns with the hearts of Fryderyk Chopin and Władysław Reymont (the urn with Chopin's heart was removed from the church during the Uprising and put into safe hiding).

Next door, No. 1 Krakowskie Przedmieście was the home of Prince Franciszek Rakoczy, the leader of rebellions for freedom in Hungary.

The Church of the Holy Cross

In front of the Staszic Palace, now the seat of the Polish Academy of Sciences, Mikołaj Kopernik has been sitting comfortably in a stone armchair since 1830. Designed by the Danish sculptor, Bertel Thorvaldsen – the author of Prince Józef Poniatowski's mounted figure – this monument, like all others in Warsaw, has had adventures. The most extraordinary one occured during the occupation in 1939–1945. First, the Germans removed from the pedestal a plaque with a Polish inscription and replaced it with another one, in German. Shortly afterwards, owing to the Polish underground the new plaque vanished. In retaliation, the occupation forces removed the statue of Jan Kiliński from its pedestal and hid it in the basement of the National Museum; the following day the following message was found on the walls of the museum: "People of Warsaw, I'm here! Jan Kiliński". In the city, leaflets were distributed, informing people that in retaliation for the removal of the Kiliński monument, the great astronomer was prolonging the winter for German armies fighting in Russia...

The Staszic Palace was built on the site of the former Church of Our Lady of Victory by Antonio Corazzi for the Society of the Friends of Science. The Russian rulers made it a medical academy, and then a Russian high school. Later, the building was redesigned in Byzantine style, and an Orthodox chapel was even placed in it. This entire Russian veneer was removed in the inter-War period – scientists returned to the Staszic Palace and the building was restored to its original look. Later, with the advent of the Second World War, the palace was burned down and subsequently rebuilt — i.e. everything occurred according to the usual cycle of events in this city.

One day, from the garret windows of the Zamoyski Palace, where Krakowskie Przedmieście joins up with Nowy Świat, several bombs were thrown onto a carriage carrying the Russian governor-general of the Polish Kingdom and the commander-in--chief of the Russian army at the time, Count Feodor Berg. In revenge, the Cossacks plundered the palace interiors and threw out onto the street the grand piano that once belonged to Chopin. At that time, the great poet Cyprian Kamil Norwid wrote the poem *Chopin's piano* and one of its lines, "Perfection took to the streets", took on a symbolic meaning for Poles.

Although it faces Krakowskie Przedmieście, the Staszic Palace is, in point of fact, part of Nowy Świat (New World) Street. Indeed, it is right here, where King's Road narrows down again, and that the next link in the chain begins.

Nowy Świat became one of the city's streets around 1650. Although, in practice, it remained for a long time a suburb in nature. While Krakowskie Przedmieście was dominated by the mansions and palaces of the landed gentry, it was wealthy Varsavian families that settled and predominated on this extension of the thoroughfare.

Nowy Świat Street

The street runs in a gentle curve towards Trzech Krzyży (Three Crosses) Square, and on, to one-time Ujazdów. In those days, it cut through the wetlands of the Kałęczyn area. The first settlers here were farmers, gardeners and craftsmen, who put up low wooden houses. In the mid-18th century, the street was cleared of mud and fodder, paved throughout its entire length. A dozen years later, seven palaces had already been built, as had the first and as yet modest town houses. The next few decades brought another thirty two-storey town houses. Pavements were laid. From the beginning of the 19th century onward, Nowy Świat became an increasingly real new world — a traditional thoroughfare. Krakowskie Przedmieście had been extended.

This link in King's Road has, at least for two centuries, also been the scene of major and extraordinary events. Royal pageants and processions of the nobility proceeded here from Castle Square towards Łazienki and Wilanów. Great patriotic demonstrations, military parades, marches through the city by foreign armies, heads of state, and the funeral processions of distinguished residents of the city and the country passed along this street. It resounds alternately with the sound of laughter and tears, music and gunfire. Carriages, cabs, and, from 1881 onwards, tramways, at first horse-driven, later electric, and — of course as soon as they were invented — motor cars have driven here. The roadway was covered successively: with paving stones, wooden cobbles, and asphalt.

Nowy Świat, now a little more dignified as it were, was, until 1939, a centre of entertainment. There were always a lot of eating places, cafés, cinemas, nightclubs, and even a circus set up just behind the street. There were also hotels, not always enjoying the highest reputation. One could mention various names, but we need not go into too much detail. As a matter of fact, out of the firms with long traditions, only the pastry shop A. Blikle remains. For a long time, it was also a fashionable cafe. It was founded in 1869 and survived all kinds of turmoil, selling its famous doughnuts to this very day.

On a slightly less entertaining note, other events occured all the time, to be commemorated for years. A leading authority on Warsaw, Stanisław Łoza, retells a dramatic moment.

"On the ground floor of the food store of the Hirszfeld Brothers, where A. Graff's toy shop had once existed (...) Between the windows, there were show-cases with toys that were covered when the shop was closed. One of these very show-cases saved me one Sunday in 1905. It was during a charge by the Hussars from Grodno on the pavements of Nowy Świat. A galloping soldier cut with his sword through a group of people who had taken refuge at the foot of the shop, but instead of hitting the people seeking refuge here, the blade of the sword left a deep scratch on the boards covering the glass pane".

Similar perils were faced by earlier and later generations, right up to the early 1980s, when young people were attacked by militia units known as ZOMO. One had to be careful in choosing the right time to take a stroll down this street, because one often risked becoming part of history, and not always on friendly terms.

After the Warsaw Uprising, when barricades were put up across Nowy Świat, the street lay almost entirely in ruins. It was rebuilt after the War in a near-perfect manner. Palaces and houses were reconstructed, many of the uglier pre-war structures were cleared away, and all buildings were kept three floors high.

Nowy Świat has slowly taken on the patina of time. Over the years, it has also grown to look more and more the way a "civilised" capital city, or a world city should look. In the inter-war years, it already was a thoroughfare in a great city. The popular Warsaw bard, Stefan Wiechecki, recalled: "Whenever I walk down Nowy Świat near Chmielna Street, I see before my eyes pre-War Warsaw, as if it were still alive. It's full of activity here. The «number nine» tram rings its bell, a cab drives out of Foksal Street in style, cars sweep past, swarms of people rush along, and the smell of valerian streams out of Malinowski's chemist shop".

Chmielna Street

Tramway No. 9 has long since disappeared, a horse-driven cab has survived in its residual state and has been transporting tourists along the route. The wind has dispersed the smell of valerian, and Malinowski's no longer exists. It is different, and not as bad as the columnist, writer, and music critic, Jerzy Waldorff put it: "Today's Nowy Świat in the evening is reminiscent of haunted catacombs (...) Not so long ago, good God... That entire city was uglier and incredibly weird, but it was lively!"

Both authors quoted above were prone to idealise a little the days of their youth, and failed to appreciate the beauty and charm of the Nowy Świat of the 1990s. After a total destruction, the street was rebuilt in the style it had at its peak. The commercial ugliness and weeds of civilisation were removed. Nowy Świat is still Warsaw's main promenade.

We shall now step off the route leading to Łazienki, the Belweder, and Wilanów, first, turning left into Ordynacka Street, and then, left again, into Jerozolimskie (Jerusalem) Avenue.

Ordynacka Street will take us to Okólnik Street. There, at No. 1 is the Baroque Ostrogski Palace (also called Castle), which houses the Fryderyk Chopin Society. This fortified building inspired many legends. One of them speaks of a golden duck swimming in an underground pond and guarding great treasures. In this palace, in 1858, the Warsaw Music Institute was founded. Lectures were given here by great Polish composers and musicians, including Stanisław Moniuszko, Zygmunt Noskowski, and Ignacy Paderewski. During the Second World War, the palace shared the fate of the city and was later detallically rebuilt in the style of the 18th-century. The Chopin Society, which operates here, organises the world-famous five-yearly International Chopin Competition at the Philharmonic Hall (the other side of Nowy Świat).

After a fleeting glance at the fairly modern headquarters of the State Music School (Okólnik 2) and the 17th-century convent of the Sisters of Charity on the escarpment, we will now return to the main route. On the way, it is worth pointing out the old location of the Krasiński Library, whose wonderful collection of manuscripts, prints, and illustrations was either taken away by the Nazis or burned (the library was rebuilt and is now open once again). Let us return to the main route.

Before reaching the intersection with Jerozolimskie Avenue, we could take another look to the left, into Foksal Street, where, in the distance, one sees the headquarters of the architects and journalists associations and their eating places; also, the little Palace of Foreign Ministry in which prime ministers and ministers visiting Poland are received. The Italian and Russian cultural institutes are also located on Foksal.

Opposite Foksal is Chmielna, one of Warsaw's traditional shopping streets, always packed with people and cars. You may not find any historical monuments here, but you can get a real taste of the atmosphere that elderly residents knew before the War.

St. Alexander's Church on Trzech Krzyży Square

Finally, the roundabout, the intersection between Nowy Świat and Jerozolimskie Avenue, and a hell-hole for motorists. To the left, there is a very large building, commonly known as the "white house", which, for years, was the main centre of power in Poland, i.e. the Central Committee of the Communist Party. Nowadays, it is home to dozens of credit institutions, including banks and the stock exchange.

The view of the Avenue is outlined by the viaduct and Poniatowski Bridge, and, beyond the massive former party headquarters, lies the National Museum and the Army Museum. The exhibits of the National Museum include a sizeable collection of Polish paintings from the 17th to the 20th century, a section of ancient art (frescos from Faras!), decorative art and numismatic sections, and many others besides. Because of limited floorspace, a large proportion of the museum's works of art are kept in storage.

But here we are now on Trzech Krzyży Square (formerly known as Golden Crosses and Alexander Square), where Nowy Świat becomes Ujazdowskie Avenue. In this square heads of state and monarchs were once welcomed and passed under triumphal gates, including Prince Józef Poniatowski.

Today, this square is known for having several cafes. In the square itself, beautiful magnolias bloom in the spring.

At its centre is St. Alexander's Church, designed by Chrystian Aigner (1826). The shrine was expanded with rather unsuccessful results at the end of the last century, and reconstructed in its "better" form after war-time destruction.

To the left, beyond the square with magnolia trees, stand the 170-year-old premises of the Institute of the Deaf and Dumb and the Blind. At the southern edge of the square, in fact at the top of Ujazdowskie Avenue, is the monument to Wincenty Witos, a peasant activist and prime minister of the Polish Republic in 1921–22, 1923, and 1926.

The avenue once referred to as Warsaw's Champs-Elysées, was created in 1731 as Calvary Road with roadside shrines of the Passion of Christ on its western flank; it led towards the wooden church of Ujazdów that existed around 1590. Later on, the little chapels, also wooden, were taken apart and replaced by trees. More or less at that time, the road became part of King Stanisław's town planning project, and took on its current name.

The avenue has adopted various styles over the last two centuries. Initially narrower, it was succesively widened. At first, on the site of today's Ujazdowski Park, a vast square was created to hold agricultural exhibitions, shows, circus performances, as well as military parades. Just beyond the park, a Russian Orthodox church was built in the late 19th century, a copy of St. Basil's on Moscow's Red Square (it was pulled down in 1922).

In the 1830s, it was highly fashionable to build residences along the Avenue. The first palaces of the aristocracy were built then. But the street became Warsaw's real showcase fifty years later. Along the section between Trzech Krzyży Square and Piękna Street, high, sturdy, but not necessarily attractive town houses were built; they neighboured upon the elegant mansions of the aristocracy and the plutocracy, all designed by famous architects, including Władysław and Leandro Marconi, Józef Dziekoński, Jan Heurich, and Józef Huss.

Small wounder then that numerous foreign embassies were set up along the Avenue after Poland regained its independence 1918, and – with an interval during the War – these (the Americans, Swiss, British, Bulgarians, Yugoslavs, and, right nearby, the Canadians and the French) have remained there until today.

During the German occupation, most Polish residents were evacuated from here, and the street was incorporated in the so-called German District. Here, at the intersection with Piękna Street, one of the boldest actions of the Second World War was carried out: soldiers of the underground National Army attacked the head of the SS and the German police, Franz Kutschera, who died on the spot. This took place on 1 February 1944. The following day, in revenge, three hundred Poles were shot dead in a public execution nearby.

For 200 years now, Ujazdowskie Avenue has remained a fashionable promenade with wide pavements, trees, the greenery of adjoining gardens, and impressive houses. The fashion has not faded for two hundred years now. However, a great deal has changed over the years. The abovementioned Ujazdowski Square has disappeared, and the fame of Swiss Valley and Bagatela has waned.

Swiss Valley was at its peak for more or less fifty years. Today it is a smallish square near Chopin Street, once an area reaching as far as Roses' Avenue (Aleja Róż). It was a centre of entertainment, concerts, a meeting place, and, later on, patriotic demonstrations and sports events were held here. The skating rink operating until the War enjoyed great popularity. Swiss Valley lasted long in the memories of the city's older rents, who refer to it as the "place beyond the city". Poets also used to seek inspiration around here.

The modern city highway, Trasa Łazienkowska, perturbed the former rhythm of Ujazdowskie Avenue, cutting through it (via a tunnel, though) at a point known as Plac na Rozdrożu (Crossroads Square). Cars zoom below in a gust of wind. I wonder whether a poet could write the following verses today:

Ujazdowskie Avenue

> "The moon from Salome's dream
> from behind the panes like silver did gleam
> From Łazienki, the Park, the Avenue fair
> The scent of the lindens wind-swept from the air".

Antoni Słonimski, the author of these words, lived in Aleja Róż and would often walk down to Belvedere or the other way to Trzech Krzyży Square, where he liked to drop in at the Actors Club on Wilcza Street. Sometimes, he would turn into Wiejska Street, in order to drink a small coffee in good company at the basement cafe of the Czytelnik publishing house. The cafe continues to be popular, although Antoni has not been there for a long time now.

Next door from the Czytelnik café (perhaps we should reverse the order here), there is a place that is crucial to the political life of the country, the unique building of the Sejm and Senate.

After this short digression, we will now return to the Avenue. We may cross the no longer quite so impressive Ujazdowski Park, and continue freely over the bridge above the traffic zooming along Trasa Łazienkowska. We now approach Ujazdowski Castle (17th-century), which was recreated from its very foundations, and cross Agrykola, a street sloping downwards, still paved until recently, and lit to this very day by gas lamps. We arrive at the entrance gate of the Botanical Gardens. We have left behind us Szuch Avenue with its grand administrative buildings such as the Ministry of Foreign Affairs and the Ministry of Education. The latter houses the Museum of Martyrdom, a place full of horrifying memories, since the Gestapo GH were located here during the last war.

Once upon a time, Varsavians used to sing: "When the lilacs bloom in the Botanical Gardens", and poems were written about the orchids and the magnolias, people arranged to meet here, and schoolchildren played truant. At the entrance to the Gardens stands the Observatory, a classical building with two observation towers. It was built in 1825 according to a design by Chrystian Aigner, Hilary Szpilowski and Michał Kado.

Some garden of this kind already existed in Warsaw earlier on, but Botanical Gardens came into being in the early 19th century on a four-and-a-half hectare piece of land portioned off from Łazienki Park.

They say it is no time to cry over roses, when forests are burning. And yet, there were so many destroyed trees and bushes to cry over, including old, valuable, and exotic ones – some displays were lost for ever, others have taken longer to recreate than those opulent palaces in the centre of town.

Monument to
Fryderyk Chopin

Lovers still meet in the shaded alleyways, at the monument to Michał Szubert, who founded the Gardens. During the Partitions, wars, and later in the period between 1982–89 (history does repeat itself after all) around the flower beds, the flower arrangements, and the ruins of the Temple of Providence, conspirators observed police officers through the roses and the tulips.

On the opposite side of Ujazdowskie Avenue, majestic buildings housing the Council of Ministers and several other major institutions stand in a disciplined line.

However, it is above all a park sprawling over an area of seventy-four hectares, whose western limit runs along the Avenue, that catches people's attention, with its landmark of the monument to Fryderyk Chopin, a work of Wacław Szymanowski, unveiled in 1926 (and naturally destroyed by the Nazis and reconstructed after the War). Concerts held there on weekend mornings enjoy great popularity.

The park's full name is The Royal Bathhouses (Łazienki Królewskie) in Warsaw. One of the most impressive public gardens in Europe, the Polish Versailles has had a rich and often sensational past.

The idyllic nature of this place – the slow and quiet pace at which people stroll along, the squeaking of pushchairs, the swans gliding along on the water, and the beautiful and colourful peacocks – conceals a dramatic past. It is however, a chronicler's annoying habit to overshadow with old memories a simple truth, namely that Łazienki, today, is a major place of leisure in the capital and is above all frequented by local residents.

Łazienki Gardens – and more precisely the palace and garden complex – has been listed under the top category of world's classified historic monuments. It has experienced many turbulent moments and has witnessed some very unusual events, as if to spite the words of a Latin inscription over the main entrance of the Palace on the Water (Pałac na Wodzie):
"This house despises grief, loves peace, recommends life in the country, and hopes to

host kind-hearted people". You only need to know the garden's history to realise that the inscription borders on irony.

Łazienki is a grand creation of King Stanisław August Poniatowski, who raised the cultural status of the city on the Vistula. It is the pearl of King's Road.

The last Polish monarch purchased from the Lubomirski princes an area then known as Ujazdów and a small woodland of Zwierzyniec (Bestiary). He turned this estate into his summer residence. And because the king had excellent taste, the residence soon turned into a great work of art. The park and the buildings situated within employed a team of the most prominent artists, engineers, and gardeners: architects Domenico Merlini and Jan Chrystian Kamsetzer; painters Marcello Bacciarelli, Jan Bogumił Plersch, and Antoni-Samuel Dąbrowski; the sculptors Andrzej Le Brun, Franciszek Pinck, G. Staggi, Tommaso Righi, the gardener Jan Chrystian Schuch. The central pivot around which everything revolved was a relatively small building, which resulted from the transformation of the so-called bathing house, a garden pavilion, into a palace.

Painters and photographers consider the Palace-on-the-Water or – as others would have it – the Palace-on-the-Isle, a subject without equal for their work. The amazingly beautiful location of this building among expanses of water and picturesque trees has enchanted visitors to the park for generations. How glorious the view onto the palace is from the monument to King Jan III Sobieski on the bridge, i.e. from Agrykola Street. The palace – and its reflection in the surrounding pond. The portico with a triangular tympanum, and statues of Achilles and Pallada. The stone vases on the balustrade. The steps leading down to the water, the stone figures of lions, and the statues of gladiators.

And from the other side – it is even more beautiful. The spacious terrace, where any self-esteeming tourist would want to take a photo. This is Warsaw's version of Piazza San Marco, Trafalgar Square, or Place de la Concorde! The sundial with the king's initials. The statues of satyrs supporting lanterns, the fountain with a basin and two 18th century sculpted compositions: stone allegories of the Vistula and the Bug rivers. And yet more statues by the great Le Brun: those of a Bacchante and a dancing satyr.

The palace itself is made up of a main body and two lateral wings added subsequently, and connected to the palace by picturesque columns spanning the canals. The architect was Domenico Merlini (while that of the original "bathing pavilion" was Tylman van Gameren), and the interiors were designed by Jan Chrystian Kamsetzer. In 1944, the Germans burned down this gem of European culture and prepared it to be blown up. The front swept through Warsaw before they had a chance to carry it out. The palace's reconstruction lasted many years after the War, and famous Polish conservation artists worked absolute marvels there.

Palace-on-the-Water in the Łazienki Park

A great deal of the furniture and artefacts that were salvaged returned to the palace, some of them unfortunately only in the form of copies, and a few objects that had not previously belonged to the Łazienki collection were also brought in. Bacciarelli's ceilings and paintings devoted to the life of King Solomon which decorated Solomon Room were lost for ever. But one should not miss the Royal Dining Room, which went down in history because of the famous royal Thursday lunches that were held there. It is also well worth taking a look at the statue of King Stanisław in the dress of a Roman emperor, by Domenico Cardelli.

One has to visit the miniature palace oneself and take in the amazing charm and the perfect geometry of this historical landmark.

From the terrace at the foot of the Palace-on-the-Water, around which the peacocks wander, one sees Łazienki's pond in all its glory. On the left hand side, one notices a structure that is unique in the world: the Amphitheatre-on-the-Isle. The stage was cut off from the audience by a strip of water, and the trees growing nearby by were combined with the theatre decor. This unusual structure was built in 1791 by Kamsetzer partly along the lines of the one that existed in ancient Herculanum. The island stage features the ancient ruins of the Roman Forum, which melted in unexpectedly well with the rubble of Warsaw's city landscape at the end of the War. Jan Lechoń, an émigré poet dying of grief for Poland where he was never to return, wrote:

"If from your ruins something remained
In this city, which is now but a new ruin
If in sinister and grim glory overshadowed
You stand there on the island on a November night
And if these days have not frightened off your Greek deities...
I know what will now be played on your stage..."

On the stage, theatrical performances, concerts, and choir singing are organised. Performances are held at various times of day, though it is especially those moonlit evenings in the open air that make an enormous impression on the audience.

At present, apart from the Palace on-the-Isle, there are eighteen other buildings of various kinds in Łazienki Park. Some of them, e.g. the Observatory, have been excluded from the limits of the park proper. But anyway, there is plenty to see.

The largest buildings in Łazienki include the Myślewicki Palace, most probably the work of Domenico Merlini (1778), and offered by the king to his nephew, Prince Józef Poniatowski. Many of the objects inside the palace sailed through the turbulent centuries, luckily, untouched. Among these, are sculptures by Jacopo Monaldi and murals by Jan Bogumił Plersch. The classical palace with an original roof based on the Chinese model, sometimes serves as a residence for foreign VIPs.

A building without which Łazienki would not be the same is the Old Orangerie. A vast amount of glass, a terrace, a stone balustrade. It too is the result of the work and talents of Merlini (1788). As the very name suggests, the building was meant to house orange trees, as it did for a while. However, the Orangerie's real highlight is the small Royal Theatre Room, one of the very rare 18th-century court theatres in the world. Its survival is a true miracle. It is hardly surprising that such a fuss is made over this room with a seating capacity of two hundred and a magnificent decor – it is only on exceptional occasions that performances are held here behind closed doors. In the main hall of the Orangerie, art or flower exhibitions as well as concerts are sometimes organised.

It is in front of this building that the monument to Prince "Pepi" – or Józef Poniatowski – stood for a while after the War.

Łazienki's White House is only two steps away. It too is one of Merlini's creations, although this is not one hundred percent certain. The little building once was the "pied-à-terre" of Mrs. Grabowska, the lady-love of the last king of Poland. It also offred temporary shelter to the future king of France, Louis XVIII, in his pre-royal days. The dining room features murals by Plersch. Nearby the villa is a sundial with a faun. One of the main characteristics of this building's interior is its central staircase. In one of the rooms, the first Polish Freemasons' lodge was formed. The king happened to be one of its members.

Amphitheatre-on-the--Isle

Not to go overboard with our obvious administration of the gardens, the other treasures have been listed in summary: the Great Outhouse, which housed, in the years of the Polish Kingdom, the Ensign School and from which a group of officer cadets left on a November night in 1830 to fight against the Russian occupation forces, thus triggering off the outbreak of a national insurrection; the Old Guardhouse by the pond, now an art gallery; the New Orangery, the New Guardhouse, once an entertainment pavilion and now the park cafe, and so many more... From the bridge on Agrykola, King Jan III Sobieski, though engrossed in his struggle against the Turks, overlooks the entire area with great serenity.

For twenty years after the Second World War efforts continued to save Łazienki from "clinical death". In the Palace on-the-Isle, 200 paintings were restored, as were 60 pieces of furniture, 17 clocks, and 80 sculptures. Some things fell even further into the chasm and – like Bacciarelli's frescos – will never be seen again.

We will now walk up the slope to the top, and back to Ujazdowskie Avenue. A last glance at the composer sitting under his weeping willow and a last farewell, as Gałczyński's put it:

The Belvedere

"An old song in a tune of old
Autumn, leaves fall from trees of gold
Are you leaving? Hmm, poor show.
Dear Lord, so far to go!
My gloves. Merci bien.
Bonsoir, monsieur Chopin".

The little square at the beginning of Bagatela (Trifle) Street got its name from an eating place that was set up there, far out of town, an inn-cum-theatre-cum-circus. Later on, it was a hospital for cholera patients. Next, it was a palace in which rich people lived. At the end of the century, a small zoo was created. Later on, it also housed a flower exhibition, a garden theatre, and finally – but this was between the two World Wars – the renowned cafe Dakowski with a summer garden. Today, it is the site of the Swedish embassy and the residence of the British ambassador.

When "entertainment" was the main activity on Bagatela Street, slightly more serious events took place just opposite the Avenue.

The Belvedere is one of the more modest Polish palaces – an embellished copy of a classical Polish mansion. The view from here must have been pretty wonderful for the building to have been given its name, from the Italian "belle vedere". The main author of the building is considered to be Fontana, while it was later renovated by Jakub Kubicki (1819–22).

This relatively small palace with beautiful geometry and a characteristic colonnade in front, is currently – as it was in the past – the seat of the president of the Polish Republic. But it has had other tennants.

Indeed, it was the residence of the Grand-Duke Konstanty, the ruler of the Russian part of Poland during the Partition. It is right here that the officer cadets from Łazienki, dressed in black capes, stole their way in on a November night. They wanted to kill the Tsarist governor-general who actually managed to get away. Later on, the palace was home to dignitaries of the Tsarist administration: Field-Marshall Ivan Paskievitch and Governor-General Hans Hartwig von Beseler. After the First World War, President

Stanisław Wojciechowski, and subsequently Marshal Józef Piłsudski moved in there; President Ignacy Mościcki established his office at the Royal Castle. At the time of publication of this book, it is President Lech Wałęsa who holds his office here.

This is where Warsaw's great King's Road, the backbone of the city, ends. However, it was more or less agreed that we would stretch it further to Wilanów which is located on an almost perfectly straight line (with one bend along the way), a couple of kilometres south of the capital. Joining Wilanów Palace to the King's Road may be justified by the fact that both its location and its history are closely associated with Warsaw.

We can get there by driving down Belwederska Street and further down its extension – Sobieski Street – which was once a narrow road lined with old trees, but is now a dual carriageway. Along the way stand modern houses and new districts whose designers do not in any way compare with the talents of Aigner or Marconi.

But here we are in Wilanów. A little off the road to Konstancin and Góra Kalwaria one notices a set of buildings that seem somewhat humble next to the magnificent gate leading to the palace and the rustling poplars in the palace gardens.

There was a time when, in the midst of this eternal murmur, a raven-haired French lady read out love letters. On the branches red squirrels frolicked, and rush leaves rustled as they rubbed against one another, while an early-evening mist rose over the backwaters. "Most delightful maiden, the one and only comfort to my heart and soul..."

The Potocki Mausoleum near Wilanów Palace

Three hundred years have gone by since the days when Maria Kazimiera Sobieska, the so-called Queen Marysieńka, imbibed the words of her loving husband, Jan III, King of Poland. The words and feelings have fluttered away, and are know common knowledge – but the rustle of the bulrushes and the poplars in the gardens along the Vistula have survived.

And so has the wonderful, melancholy, though highly popular, isolated yet suburban palace, the most beautiful Baroque aristocratic residence in Poland. Experts consider it one of the treasures of world culture. Ordinary citizens of this country as well as foreign visitors cross Wilanów's gate with greater or lesser gaps in their education, but always leave in great awe.

Over the front doors of the palace, shine the sharp flames of a golden sun. *Refulsit Sol in Clipeis* – the sun blazed on the shields, the inscription says. The shields are the coat of arms of the Sobieskis, while the sun is a symbol of power.

The Polish monarch, Jan Sobieski, remained forever a knight from the borderlands of Poland. In the Wilanów rushes, he hunted for herons (where are they now?). Then, in 1677, out of nostalgia for the Podolian meadows and gullies, he acquired Wilanów (then still called Milanów) as his suburban property. The very modest manor house with a flower and vegetable garden soon changed, thanks to the most skillful artists, into a royal residence on a par with Vienna's Belvedere and as stately as England's Windsor Castle. With the help of their patron's good taste and wisdom, the architects based their design on that of Italian Baroque villas, and that of the Roman villa Doria Pamphili, in particular.

Later on, as we well know, it was just like in the popular song: *And when the king went to war...* To a distant, bloody, and difficult war with an Asian power. Jan had experienced numerous battles, but this one had no equal. At the head of the combined armies of Central Europe, he won, at Vienna's Kahlenberg, his famous victory against the Turkish army of Kara Mustafa. It is from there, from a field tent, that he sent his letters to Marysieńka.

One might venture to say that the victory in Vienna and the construction of Wilanów Palace were Jan III's two historic achievements. As for the signifance and historic consequences of the former, opinions vary, while the latter is considered an unquestionable success by all.

Wilanów is one of the few European palaces, and perhaps the only one besides Wawel, where a rich, creative, and artistic project was implemented in a deliberate and consistent manner. The elements in the artistry and decorative sculptures were made to fit the architectural plans. The greatest art masters of Europe at the time were responsible for the end result: the architect Agostino Locci, the sculptors Andreas Schluter and Stefan Szwaner, the stucco artist and architect Józef Bellotti, the painters Jerzy Szymanowicz-Siemiginowski, Claude Callot, Michelangelo Palloni. As one can see, Poland's king did not suffer from xenophobia; he was, as Stanisław August proved to be one century later, a real connoisseur and patron of the arts.

The human scale of Wilanów is captivating. The palace is not monumental and gives the impression of being constantly lived in. There are almost always freshly cut flowers in the vases, clean curtains in the windows, clocks striking the hour on time...

Wilanów Palace from the east

Genius loci lives on in the palace and has not been chased away by the electroluxes and other gadgets of modern-day civilisation. In many rooms, one senses the presence of good spirits, and the more sensitive can apparently fell the constant presence of the king himself, who died here one June night in 1696.

The value of this Baroque residence is determined by its architecture as well as the great artistry that went into building it, including the magnificent frescos, some of which were not discovered till after the War.

But newcomers are most touched by that "lived-in feel to the place", an atmosphere of privacy in what is, after all, a public building.

Only the priviledged few were ever invited to stay there. The guest rooms in the right, 19th-century wing of the palace have played host to Italian President Giuseppe Saragat, Ethiopian Emperor Haile Selasie, the Shah of Iran, the king of Morocco, Leonid Brezhnev, Charles de Gaulle (the bed had to be lengthened for him by half a metre).

When one stands in the Royal Bedroom, in the dining room of August II, the bathing apartments of Princess Lubomirska, the historical continuity of these interiors seems to have remained uninterrupted for centuries.

Wilanów got off lightly in recent historical events, inasmuch as... its walls remained. The interiors were plundered, the garden constructions and statues were obliterated, the park was 90%-destroyed. Restoration work on the building lasted until 1964, while its collections took even longer to retrieve.

All of this sounds a little fantastic, when one stands in springtime by a lawn covered with crocuses, set against the dazzlingly white walls of the royal residence. What significance could a mere two or three decades have in the centuries-long existence of such a palace?...

Wilanów Palace

Warsaw is not a trivial city. Although King's Road and everything that is situated along it has been mentioned here with great pride, one has to say openly: as far as artistic splendour is concerned, the Polish metropolis falls far short of many of its counterparts elsehwhere in the world. When looking for sources of prestige in the city, its place within the hierarchy of centres of European culture, one should emphasize the uniqueness of Poland's capital: for centuries, works of art and architecture shared the fate of its people. Together they were born, together they lived, and together they died. The artistic criteria in evaluating dead sculptures often give way to emotional ones, and sometimes become subordinate to them. The monument to Nicolas Copernicus is not only important because it portrays the great astronomer and was created by an outstanding sculptor – it is close to everything in this city, because it shared good and bad times alike, and had both a wonderful and a terrible past, one which is – as is the case with the city as a whole – quite simply sensational.

Only a poet like Czesław Miłosz could express what lies so deep within:

> "This country has its planets and rivers
> But it is as frail as the edge of the morning.
> It is we who create it daily anew
> Respecting more what is real
> Than what in name and sound has turned to stone.
> And so, parforce, we snatch it from the world,
> Or else, too easy, it does not exist at all.
> Farewell, things past. The echo is still calling (...)"

The façade of the early 15th-century Church
of the Visitation of Our Lady

The escarpment at New Town. From the right, the
churches of the Visitation of Our Lady, the Sisters of
the Holy Sacrament, and St. Benon's

The late 17th-century Church of the Holy Sacrament
on New Town Market Square, designed by Tylman
van Gameren

House on Freta Street
where Maria Skłodowska-Curie
was born

Freta Street

Mostowa Street

Early 18th-century
Pauline Church of the Holy Spirit

The Barbican fortifications, built in the 15th
century and dismantled in the 18th, and reconstructed
before the Second World War

◄ Old Town Market Square

Kamienne Schodki

The Zakrzewski side
of Old Town Market Square

Fragments of façades on Old Town Market Square:
◄ Frieze with Saturnalia (18th-century), head of a black
boy on the 18th-century town house,
Pod Murzynkiem. 16-century statues of the Holy
Virgin, St. John and St. Anne

Old Town Market Square from Świętojańska Street

The Old Town Market

Wąski Dunaj Street

Świętojańska Street

St. Martin's Church on Piwna Street

Last dukes of Mazovia: Stanisław (1501—1524)
and Janusz (1502—1526) resting in the Cathedral

Grave of Primate Cardinal Stefan Wyszyński,
who died in 1981

Caterpillar tracks of a nazi tank that blew up
the Cathedral walls during the Warsaw Uprising
in 1944

Front of St. John's Cathedral (late 13th/early 14th
◄ century)

Kanonia Street

The Old Town, from Podwale

Castle Square, view onto Krakowskie
Przedmieście

Town houses on Castle Square

The Royal Castle

Chapel at the Royal Castle

The King's Dressing-Room

Chamber with two pillars

The Audience Hall ▶

The Marble Room. Portrait of
Stanisław August Poniatowski in
ceremonial dress designed by
M. Bacciarelli

Knights' Hall; statue of Chronos
(J. Monaldi, 1784–1786)

Senate Hall where
the 3rd May
Constitution 1791
was proclaimed

Canaletto Room

Fragment of Canaletto's *Warsaw Panorama* of 1770 (view from Praga)

Castle Square

Monument to the Polish
king, Zygmunt III Vasa
(Clemente Molli; 1644)

◄ Castle Square

Fragment of the East-West Highway running under
King's Road

The East-West Highway

St. Anne's Church

Miodowa Street

Primates' Palace

The Civic Club

Town houses on Krakowskie
Przedmieście

Figure of Our Lady of Passau
commemorating Jan III Sobieski's
victory in Vienna; Józef Bellotti, 1683

Interior of the chemists' shop, "On the Royal Way"

Adam Mickiewicz Monument created by Cyprian Godebski in 1898

Carmelite Church of the Ascension of Our Lady.
◄ The church's late 17th-century central altar designed
by Tylman van Gameren

The 17th-century Radziwiłł Palace, now the seat
of the Council of Ministers

Monument to Prince Józef Poniatowski
by Bertel Thorvaldsen (1832)

The mid-18th-century Church of the Visitation Nuns

Church of the Visitation Nuns. Pulpit designed
by Jan Plersch

Monument to Primate Stefan Wyszyński

Guardhouse at the Potocki Palace

Potocki Palace, now housing the Ministry of Culture and Art

Kozia Street

Town house where Kozia Street joins Krakowskie Przedmieście

Monument to the Heroes
of Warsaw, by Zygmunt
Konieczny (1964)

Façade of the opera house
designed by Antonio Corazzi
in 1825—1836

Productions at Teatr Wielki: Richard Wagner's
opera *The Gold of the Rhine* and a ballet
to Mieczysław Karłowicz's musical poem,
Stanisław and Anna Oświęcim

Victoria Hotel

Europejski Hotel

Bristol Hotel

Krakowskie Przedmieście at Warsaw University

Bookstall in front of the University

Tyszkiewicz Palace with Atlas figures created
by Andrzej Le Brun (18th-century)

The Main Gate of the University

Eagle crowning the main University gate

Inauguration ceremony of the academic year at the University

The University Library

One of the exhibition rooms at Zachęta Art Gallery

Zachęta building designed by Stefan Szyller in 1903

The 18th-century Czapski Palace, now housing the Fine Arts Academy

The drawing room of the Chopin family in the left wing of the Academy building

The painting department of the Fine Arts Academy

Krakowskie Przedmieście seen from the Church of the Holy Cross ►

The Staszic Palace designed by Antonio Corazzi
in 1820—1823, now the headquarters of the Polish
Academy of Sciences

A youth happening at the Copernicus Monument
(created by Bertel Thorvaldsen in 1830)

Church of the Holy Cross designed by
Józef Bellotti in 1662–1696

Figure of Christ by Andrzej Pruszyński in 1858
in front of the Church of the Holy Cross

Epitaph with the heart of Fryderyk Chopin

The Ostrogski Palace by Tylman van Gameren. Built in 1681—1685, now the headquarters of the Fryderyk Chopin Society

Fryderyk Chopin, aged 19. Painting by A. Mierosławski

Fryderyk Chopin, aged 28. Painting by Eugène Delacroix

Interior of the museum with Chopin's last piano

A gallery on Chmielna Street

Professor Andrzej Blikle, a co-owner of Blikle's pastry shop, founded in 1863

Nowy Świat near Ordynacka Street

◄ View of Nowy Świat towards Świętokrzyska Street

The General Charles de Gaulle Roundabout

The former building of the Central Committee of the
Communist Party, now home to banking institutions

Trzech Krzyży Square

St. Alexander's Church with the figure
St. John Nepomucen (1756) on
Trzech Krzyży Square

The Polish parliament, or Sejm

The eastern and western sides
of Ujazdowskie Avenue

Doorway to the Strzałecki's house
"Pod Gigantami" on Ujazdowskie Avenue

Part of Ujazdowskie Avenue with the Wielopolski
Mansion (left), now housing the British Embassy

The Sobański Mansion with a copy of 15th-century
sculpture of David by Donatello

The Poznański Mansion

The Łazienkowska Highway at Na Rozdrożu Square

Ujazdowski Castle

The Council of Minister's building

The Botanical Gardens

A Chopin concert in Łazienki

Fragment of the Fryderyk Chopin Monument, created by Wacław Szymanowski in the early 20th century

◄ Palace-on-the-Water in the Łazienki Park
(late 18th century), designed by Domenico Merlini

The Landscape Room in Myślewicki Palace

Interiors in the Palace-on-the-Water in Łazienki

The Portrait Gallery and the Ballroom at the Palace-on-the-Water

Sundial from 1777 in front of the
Palace-on-the-Water

One of the many squirrels in Łazienki

Monument to the Polish king, Jan III Sobieski,
created in 1788 by Franciszek Pinck

Amphitheatre with its stage on an island, built on the lines of the theatre in Herculanum

St. Anne's Church in Wilanów

The Potocki Mausoleum near Wilanów Palace

Wilanów Palace, built by King Jan III Sobieski
in the late 17th century ▶

The King's Antechamber

The Sobieski Family, 18th-century painting;
author unknown

The Red Room

The bathroom of the Princess Lubomirska
and the Queen's Bedroom at Wilanów Palace

Part of Wilanów Park

Palace tower with Atlas lifting a globe

A fronton of Sybil on the southern façade of the palace

Eros sitting on a sphinx; an 18th-century garden sculpture

Sundial on one of the façades of Wilanów Palace

Bas-relief from 1725 depicting Bacchus and Erigone

Wilanów Palace from the east ►

La Petite Prague

LA VIST